STORY OF MY LIFE

Mom's

Legacy Journal & Memory Keepsake Workbook

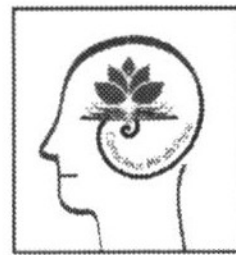

Conscious Minds Press

For all those families with stories to tell.

May your voices be heard.

May your heart's resonance be felt.

May your learning & wisdom carry on.

Let these words you write
inform, heal, and allow the next
generations to evolve for the betterment
of themselves and the all.

Contents

The following sections will help you compile a complete life story memoir that you can be proud to share with those you love.

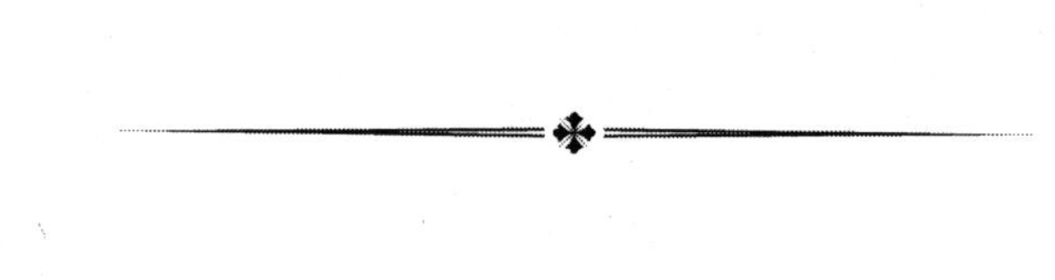

There often comes a time in one's life that sharing more of who you are - what made you the person you are today, where you came from, what you endured and overcame, and all the experiences and lessons you've learned - are yearning to be passed on. That and of course the favorite family recipes, long told stories of certain people in the family, and so many other things are important to keeping the family history alive.

Looking back over a lifetime can be overwhelming. Trying to capture the meaningful information in an organized and engaging way even more daunting. This legacy workbook will hold your hand throughout the task of telling the story of your life. The framework of the book will help you both recall and share things clearly so that you'll end up with a legacy keepsake you'll be proud to pass on to the next generations.

This creation is more than just a book of stats and depiction of events. It is a portrayal of a life lived through your eyes and heart. It is a sharing of experiences, passions, values, hopes, dreams, and belief in the importance of family history.

The workbook has been divided into to several sections to help you organize your life in a meaningful way. Many prompts will guide you through the creation process however there are spaces for own unique additions as each person's life has its nuances that are important to share. There are also many places to add photos or share other important memorabilia for the family.

If you come across any questions that don't apply to your life, skip them. If you can't remember something fully, pencil in what you do and come back to it when you know more. Once you start committing to this process, you'll be surprised at how many memories start flooding back. An event you recall may remind you of an important person that impacted your life in some way, which makes you think about an important value in life that became a guiding principle you'd like to pass on. The more you allow the process to organically unfold, the more enjoyable this project will be.

Why do this...

You are about to undergo an important and fulfilling project - creating the story of your life. This is an undertaking that will be rewarding personally and will also have many positive impacts with those you choose to share it. Remembering why you are taking the time to complete this book will be a helpful motivator to keep going when you're feeling stuck. Here's a few reasons why you might undertake this project:

Self Awareness and Personal Growth

The process of self reflection and introspection can be really helpful in making sense of your experience of life. Why you made the choices you did and why you feel the way you do. By reflecting on the past, you can start to see the patterns, themes, and lessons learned that shaped your personality, created your life situation, and honed your worldview.

Preserving History and Memories for Others

The art of sharing history through storytelling is becoming lost. Families are more geographically and structurally diverse than ever before. Much of what got us to who we are today will get lost along the way unless we consciously choose to share it.

Documenting your life story helps preserve important family history and memories for future generations. This book becomes a tangible legacy that allows children, grandchildren, great grandchildren and so forth to connect to the family roots which impact who they are and will become. You have a particular point of view and impact on the family history that deserves to be told.

Strengthen Connections

Sharing your story can strengthen your relationships with others. It can encourage deeper conversations and more empathy between family members. It can also foster a sense of belonging and appreciation for the family in a new way.

You can even work with other family members in helping to complete this book. It can bring you closer as you share about your life in a way perhaps you haven't before. Let your kids or grandkids ask you the questions and help you fill in the spaces if you need support.

Writing can Heal and Give Closure

Writing about ourselves and experiences, both the good and the challenging ones, can be very therapeutic. It can help us to process emotions, gain clarity and find closure. The journaling industry is huge because it is a proven helpful tool. Sharing your story can help inspire and empower others. It can give other family members understanding to patterns and dynamics that will allow them more compassion and choice in how they engage and move forward in life. Sometimes it can be easier to write what we want to share about ourselves when we can't seem to say it out loud.

Remembering How Far We've Come

Over a lifetime we can often forget the key moments that got us to where we are today. This book allows you to celebrate all your achievements and milestones along the way. You may be surprised to see how much of an impact your life has made and how the path you forged has influenced the next generations. Not only will you find joy, self-worth and fulfillment in this writing process, but you will also inspire and motivate others to consciously create their own legacy.

Writing your life story is a powerful act of self-discovery, healing, and connection. Your impact on the family legacy is worth sharing. It can have an immensely positive affect on yourself and all those who receive it.

Overcoming Challenges

Writing your life story can be rewarding, but it will also be a challenging endeavor at times. This book has been designed to help you every step along the way. Here are a few general challenges you might encounter and how to overcome them:

Yikes! I Can't Remember

- Use memory aids like photos, yearbooks, journals, and personal documents to help you.
- Things that involve your senses can help trigger memories. Expose yourself to scents, music, or objects associated with certain people or places to help your memories flow.
- Revisit significant locations like childhood home, schools, favorite hangouts of past, or others places of that events took place. Pay attention to thoughts, feelings and other details that arise.
- Talk with family and friends about shared experiences and get them to give their perspective on those times and events.
- Use creative activities like drawing, painting, or crafting to help open up your mind. It activates a different part of your brain that can help with memory recall.
- Watch movies or read books from the time period you are exploring or that relate to the subject you are trying to recall. Pay attention to how it resonates with your own experience.
- Just start journaling and see what comes to surface. You may recall things better when you take the pressure off a particular subject.
- Let yourself off the hook. Memory gaps are normal. Focus on what you can remember and let go of the need for perfect accuracy. You can always pencil something in and then come back to it when you remember more.

It's Too Emotional

Times in our past that are traumatic or painful can bring up strong emotions.

- Create a supportive environment for writing and reminiscing.
- Take your time. Focus on challenging areas as you feel ready.
- Give yourself permission to feel your emotions and prioritize self-compassion. Being radically honest about yourself and your story can bring up feelings of vulnerability.
- Do self care like meditation, walks in nature, or take a soothing bath. Reach out to supportive friends. Speak with a therapist if you need more help processing unresolved trauma or emotions. It's never too late to release yourself from past pain.
- Choose not to share about a specific time or topic. This is your story. You can share as much as you feel comfortable.

Overwhelming Task

- This is a project that is meant to be tackled over time. Choose to start with areas of focus that are easier to complete or are fun to write about. This will get you started and give you momentum to complete the rest.
- Set goals. Make time each week or month to write or complete a section. Focusing one step at a time will soon carry you to completing the whole book.
- Along with setting realistic writing goals, focus on your progress rather than perfection. Give yourself and your story the freedom to be what it is.
- Seek encouragement and support from friends and family to gain motivation and confidence when needed.

What's the Truth

- This book is about sharing your experience and interpretation of events rather than regurgitating a bunch of data and facts.
- Accepting there may be multiple points of view of any particular situation is helpful. You can choose to incorporate the viewpoints of other people about any memory to give a more encompassing log of the event.

STORY
OF
MY LIFE

Name:

Date Written: ____________________

Why I'm Writing This

Letting others know why you decided to take on this project will help give them context to its importance not only to you but the family. Do you want them to understand you better than you were able to communicate in life? Do you want to preserve family history so that it isn't lost over time? Do you hope to inspire others in the family to write their own story? Whatever your reasons, sharing them will help you keep motivated in completing this book and will motivate others to engage in helping you along the way. At the very least they know why it was important to you to share this information with them.

What motivated you to document your life story?

What are your hopes and expectations for this project?

ABOUT
me

BORN (M/D/YR):

TIME:

LOCATION:

NAME GIVEN:

How did your parent's pick your name?

Do you like your given name?

Were you told any memorable stories about your birth?

EYE COLOR:

HAIR COLOR:

HEIGHT:

OTHER NOTABLE FEATURES:

Do you resemble anyone in the family?

CURRENT CITY OF RESIDENCE:

OTHER PLACES YOU'VE LIVED:

MY FAVORITES

Color
Flower
Food
Scent
Movie/TV Show
Place
Person
Way to Spend the Day
Holiday
Desert
Game
Hobby
Animal
Home

Photos of little me...

My Early Years & Family Background

MY EARLY YEARS & FAMILY BACKGROUND

As you start exploring your childhood years, it is impossible not to include your family background and dynamics. Who we are is first shaped by our family upbringing, influences, and experiences. The questions in this section help you dive into your early years.

Really early childhood memories are often not accessible so you may rely on stories you've been told about your younger years. If you have parents still alive, you may want to ask them some questions to help complete this section. Pulling out old photo albums and memory books can be helpful.

The aim of this section to paint a vivid picture of the environment in which you grew up. Here you will share some memorable moments from your childhood, talk about some the most influential people in your younger years and explore some of the family tree from which you grew.

Here's a simple family tree to get you started. Families can get complex - adjust as needed. There are free genealogy mapping services online if you want to build out a full map to print and put with this book. Space has been allotted for future grandchildren.

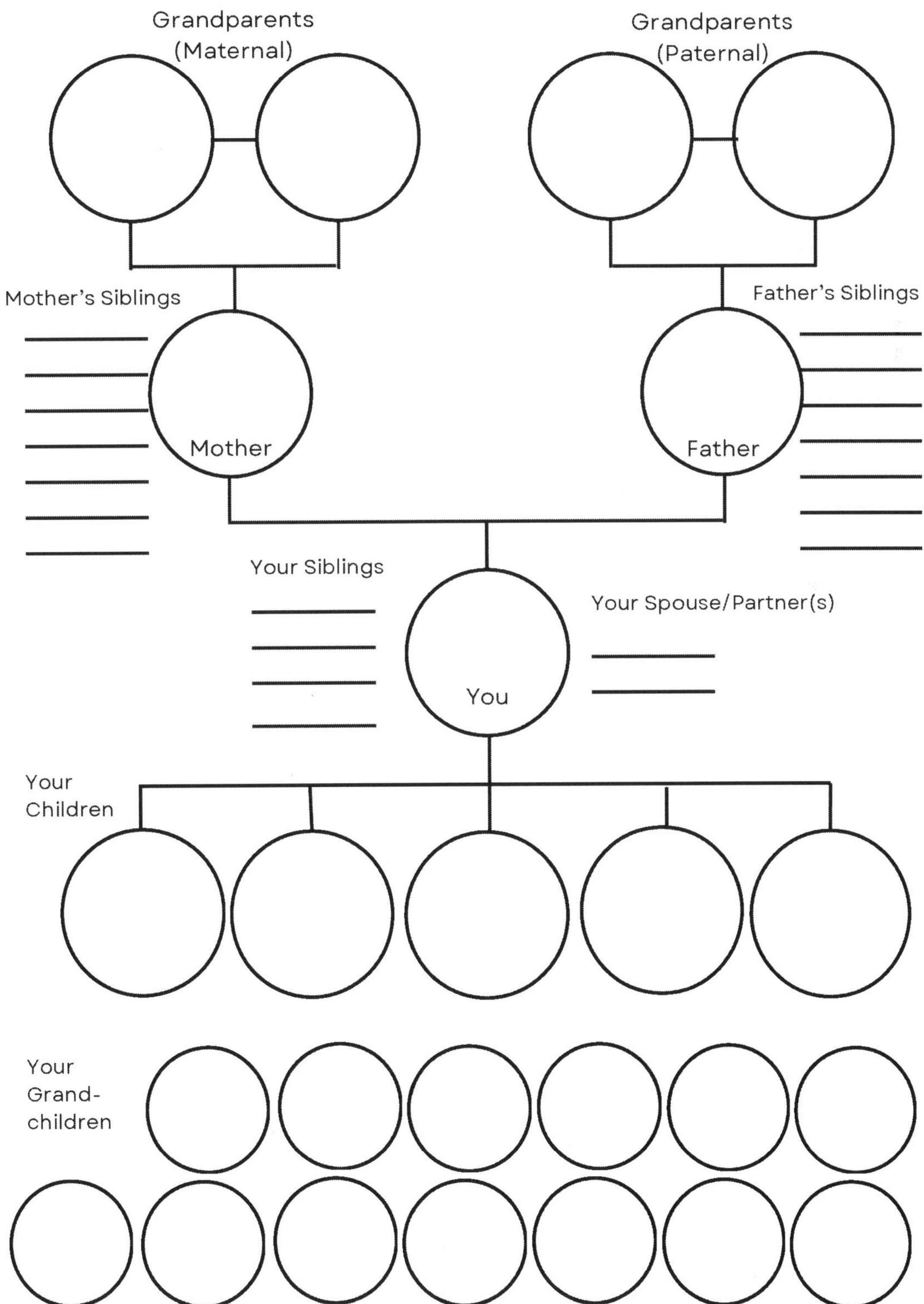

Family Background

How did being born into this position in the family tree affect you and the family? If you had siblings, were they excited for your arrival?

What was it like growing up where you did? If you moved locations describe how that impacted you for better or worse.

What was the atmosphere like in your household growing up?

What were the cultural or religious traditions that were important to the family?

How did you celebrate holidays?

How much were extended family included in your life - aunts, uncles, cousins, etc.

Upbringing

What were some of your childhood memories that stand out in your mind in the following age brackets?

Ages 0 - 5 years

Ages 6 - 10 years

BEST MOMENT

Ages 11 - 15 years

MY LIFE

Ages 16 - 19 years

Pictures of my younger years...

If you had to sum up the essence of your upbringing, how would you describe it?

Were there any particular challenges your family faced when you were a child?

What were the expectations of you as a member of the family? Were there certain ways you need to be or things you had to do to contribute to the family unit?

How were you rewarded or punished for certain behaviours?

What were your first words?

What was your bedroom like?

Did you have any childhood pets?
What were they and their names?

Did you have a favorite song or band?

What was your first car you owned?

How did you learn to drive a car?

What is a family vacation that stands out in your memories?

Do you remember your first love/crush?

Impactful People

Who were the most influential people in your life as a child? This might be a family member, teacher, neighbor, friend... How did they impact your life?

What lessons or wisdom did you gain in childhood that made a lasting impact throughout your life. What happened? Who was involved? What did you learn and how did it shape you?

Early Education & Interests

What was your experience like in school? From primary to high school? Share any stand out moments or memories.

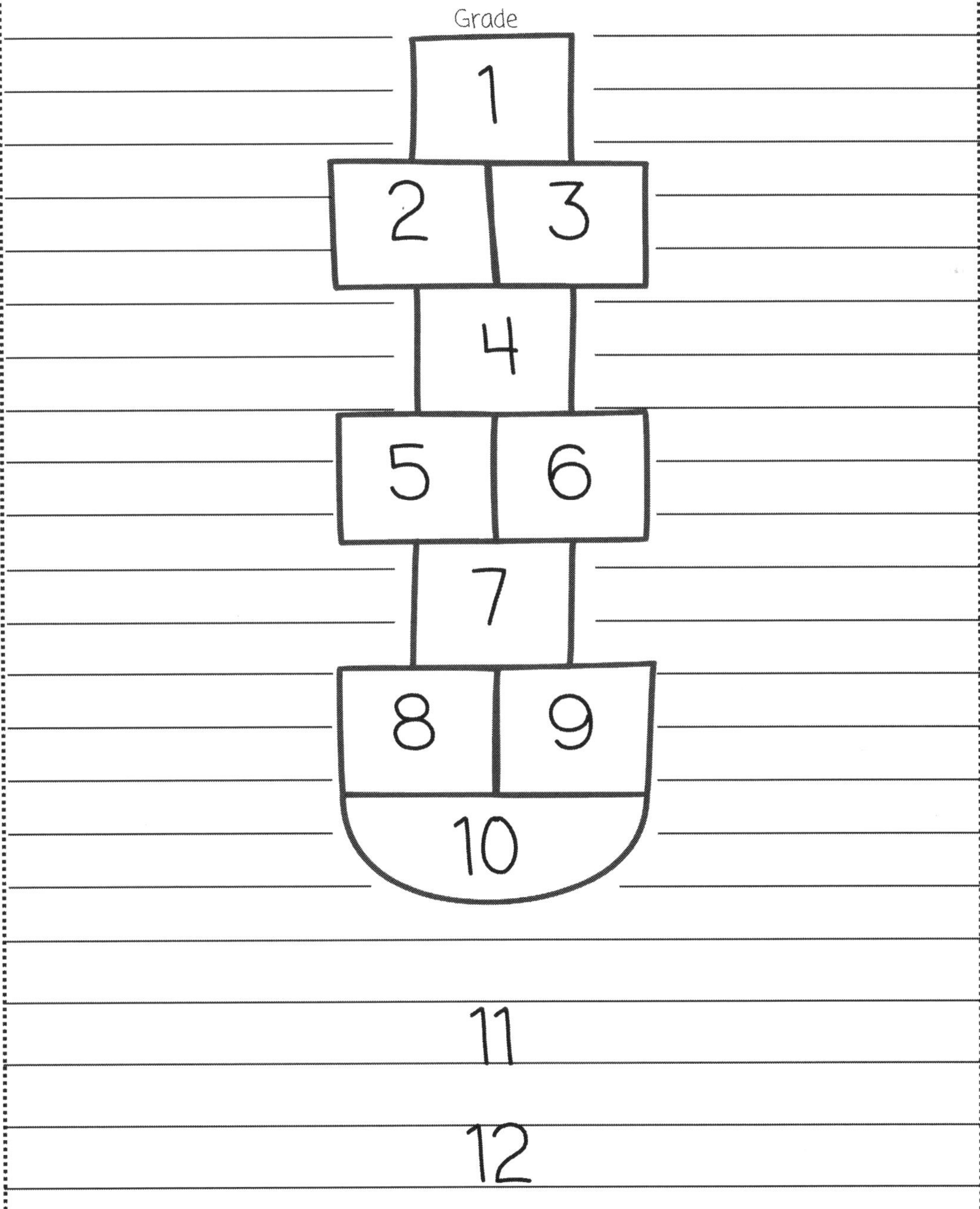

11

12

Did your experience of school drastically change throughout the years? Why or why not?

What were your favorite subjects?

What activities did you like the most and least in school?

Memorable school trips? Where did you go? What happened?

Did you have any favourite teachers or mentors? If so, what makes them special or memorable?

What did you love to do as a child? Did you have any passions, interests, or hobbies?

Did you have any favorite toys or games as a child?

Do you remember having any dreams about what you wanted to become in life?

Memorable Moments & Places

What specific events or experiences from your childhood stand out in your mind as particularly memorable or significant in some way? Ex. a special birthday, school event, family reunion, wedding, family trip, or some other non event specific moment of importance in some way - a memorable moment with a friend, an encounter with an animal or even an experience with the bullies at school.

What lessons or insights did those moments give you that have stayed with you over the years? How have they influenced who you are today?

Did you have any special places you like to be in or go to? Ex. favorite tree fort, the window seat in your room, your uncle's farm.

How did you make pocket money? Did you sell lemonade, cut lawns for the neighbors, get paid for helping with chores around the house?

When did you get your first job? What was it? What was your motivation to get a job? What did you do with the money?

Family Dynamics

How would you describe the dynamics in your family growing up?

What family values or principles were emphasized?

How did the family handle challenge, conflict, or other tensions?

What did the family like to do together?

Are there any particular stories about family members that stick out in your memory?

Higher Education & Career

This section helps you explore your later years educational experience, career path(s), achievements, challenges, and reflections on your professional life. You will explore pivotal moments and experiences that shaped your career path including the education and events that landed you there.

Tip 1: If you didn't complete any additional education you can skip those pages. Education can include those learnings you received outside a formal schooling institute like a college or university.

Tip 2: You may not consider your chosen work a career however in the context of this book we do. You can share about important jobs you held or various work you've done in this career section.

Education Experience

What was your educational experience like beyond high school? Did you attend any colleges or universities? Did you do any apprenticeships or other learning?

School Name
Location
Dates
Focus of Study

School Name
Location
Dates
Focus of Study

School Name
Location
Dates
Focus of Study

Did you have any memorable teachers or mentors during this time period?

Did you face any challenges in your educational experiences? What were they and how did you overcome them?

Were there any important people that influenced your life at that time? Ex. dorm buddy, best friend, family member...

Career Path & Milestones

How did you decide on your chosen career or work path? Share any pivotal moments that shaped your career decisions - interests, passions, other events.

How did your career path and goals evolve over time?

If you could go back in time, would you change anything?

Describe some of your most memorable experiences or achievements professionally.

Are there any defining moments or projects that stand out in your mind?

What challenges did you face on your career path and how did you overcome them?

How have you contributed to your professional growth? Ex. additional education, training, skill development, self study

Did you have any mentors or other allies that contributed to your career growth?

Reflections on Work/Life

How to you feel you handled balancing work with family, hobbies, and other areas of your life?

What have you learned about maintaining work life balance?

Are there any actions or decisions you regret with regards to work?

Looking back on your work life, what are some of the most valuable lessons you've learned and want to share?

What advice would you like to leave about following a similar path to your work/career?

“A picture is worth a thousand words”...

Personal Relationships

This section explores the personal relationships of family, friends, spouses/partners, children and pets. Personal relationships and interpersonal experiences shape our life in many ways which can impact future generations as well. Start to consider those relationships that have profoundly impacted your life in some way. In this section you will provide insight into the dynamics, challenges and lessons learned from the people in your life.

You will be exploring the following relationships:

- Family Relationships (parents, grandparents, siblings, aunts, uncles, cousins)
- Friendships
- Romantic Relationships (partners, spouses)
- Parenting & Children
- Beloved Pets
- Other Support Systems
- Relationship Dynamics
- In Memoriam

Family Relationships

Describe your relationship with each of your family members - grandparents, parents, siblings, and important extended family members (aunts, uncles, cousins).

Consider the following questions for each of them:

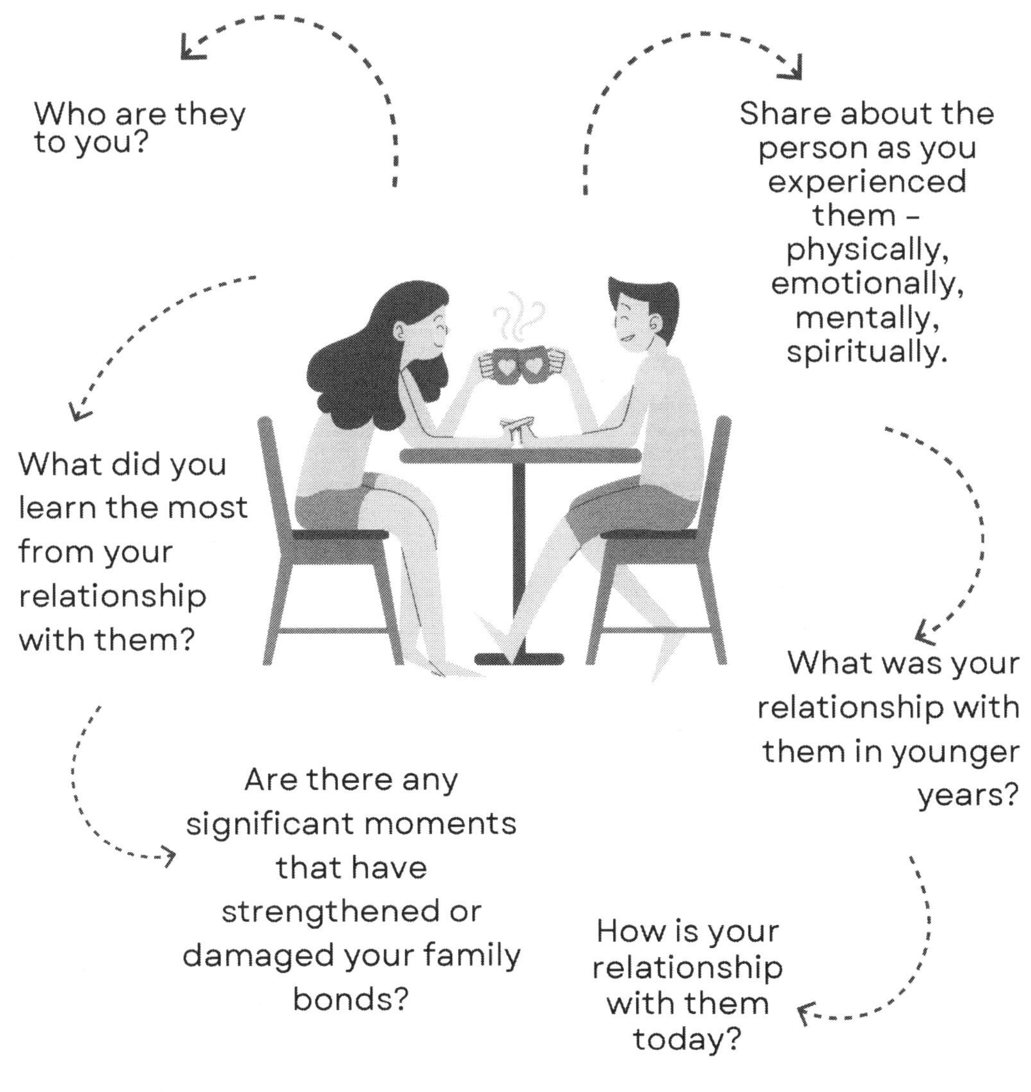

Name: Relationship:

Name: Relationship:

Name: Relationship:

Name: Relationship:

Name: Relationship:

Name: Relationship:

Name: Relationship:

Name: Relationship:

Name: Relationship:

Name: Relationship:

Name: Relationship:

Name: Relationship:

Name: Relationship:

Name: Relationship:

My favorite family photos...

Friendships

Share about some of your closest friendships throughout life that have made a significant difference to your journey. How have your relationships evolved over time?

What lessons have you learned from the challenges or conflicts you've experienced with friends?

What do you consider the more important qualities in a friendship?

What type of friend have you aspired to be? Do you think you have achieved it?

My friends and me...

Romantic Relationships

Share about the most significant romantic relationships that have influenced your life.

How did you meet your current partner/spouse?

If you had only a few minutes to share some final words with your current partner/spouse, what would you say to them?

What has been your experience with romantic love and how has that evolved over time?

What is your perspective on commitment and the keys to a successful partnership?

Love and Life.

Parenting & Children

Can you summarize your experience as a parent? What have you enjoyed the most and what have you found most challenging?

How did your perspective and experience of life change when you became a parent?

How would you describe each of your children and what lessons did you learn from each of them?

Name:

Name:

Name:

Name:

Name:

Name:

Do you have any favorite parenting memories?

What values or lessons do you hope you instilled in your children?

Grandparenting

This section on grandparenting has been included so you can add to it if/when it becomes relevant.

Can you summarize your experience as a grandparent? What have you enjoyed the most and what have you found most challenging?

How did your perspective and experience of life change when you became a grandparent?

Do you have any favorite grandparenting memories?

What values or lessons do you hope you instilled in your grandchildren?

How would you describe each of your grandchildren and what lessons did you learn from each of them?

Name:

Name:

Name:

Name:

Name:

Name:

Name:

Name:

Name:

The kids & grandkids & me.

Beloved Pets

Some of the most influential relationships we have in our life can be with our cherished pets. Who are the beloved animals that have been in your life?

Describe your relationship with the animals of your life. What did they mean to you? How did they affect your life?

What have you learned from your personal relationship with animals that you would like to pass on to others?

Beloved pets of the years...

Other Support

Who have you been able to lean on when times have been challenging?

How have you built your support system over the years?

Relationship Learnings

How have you tried to create healthy relationships with others?

What have you learned about yourself through your relationships with others?

Relationship Learnings

Share any particular impactful moments in relationships that altered your perspective or path in life.

What patterns in relationships have you noticed run in the family, with your friendships, or in romantic relationships?

In Memoriam

Mark the passing of an important friend, family member, beloved pet, etc. by mentioning them here. Include pictures or other memorabilia.

In Memoriam

Mark the passing of an important friend, family member, beloved pet, etc. by mentioning them here. Include pictures or other memorabilia.

In Memoriam

Mark the passing of an important friend, family member, beloved pet, etc. by mentioning them here. Include pictures or other memorabilia.

The Challenges I've Faced

We all go through ups and downs in life. By exploring our challenges we can see the lessons learned and how they ultimately shaped our life to be what it is today.

Sharing how we navigated life can help others to gain understanding, have compassion, and even find inspiration for their own life. This is a place to see your resilience and witness your personal growth journey.

Personal Challenges

What are some of the biggest challenges you have faced in life? How did you cope with them and what did you learn in the process? Consider the emotional, mental, physical and spiritual impacts.

Professional Challenges

What obstacles did you face in your professional life? How did you navigate them and what did you learn? How did those moments shift your career/work focus?

Health Challenges

What significant health challenges or illnesses have you experienced? When did they happen? How did they affect your life?

Who supported you with your health and wellbeing?

Financial Challenges

Have you faced any financial setbacks or significant challenges? What happened? When?

How did you overcome them?

How did those experiences change you or the way you live your life?

Relationship Challenges

What significant relationship conflicts have occurred that changed you in some way.

How were you able to navigate through the challenges?

Were you able to find resolution?

What did you learn about yourself and others as a result of those difficult times?

Lessons in Overcoming

What strengths and resources have you learned you possess that helped you to overcome challenges in life?

Are there any particular situations you are especially proud of overcoming?

What advice can you give others facing similar challenges in life?

Milestones & Achievements

MILESTONES & ACHIEVEMENTS

No doubt you have achieved many things across many areas of your life. Whether seemingly big or small, together they are part of what has made you the person you are today. This section is to provide some insights into what you have accomplished, your motivations, and contributions to work, community, and self. You could view these as defining moments in your life.

Use the space on the following page to note these achievements:

PERSONAL ACHIEVEMENTS

What are you proud you accomplished in life - personal growth and mindset changes, turning points in health, stopping of a family pattern, etc.

CAREER ACHIEVEMENTS

What work accomplishments would you like to celebrate?

EDUCATIONAL ACHIEVEMENTS

What learning milestones or academic achievements are you proud of?

PASSIONS ACHIEVEMENTS

Where have you achieved accolades through your passions - artist creations, sporting endeavors, gaming pursuits, etc.?

COMMUNITY/VOLUNTEER CONTRIBUTIONS

In what ways have you given back to others? Where did you choose to contribute your time or money, and why?

Any other awards or notable achievements you would like to have remembered by others.

My Achievements

PERSONAL ACHIEVEMENTS

WINS

CAREER ACHIEVEMENTS

AWARDS

EDUCATIONAL ACHIEVEMENTS

MILESTONES

PASSION ACHIEVEMENTS

RECOGNITION

COMMUNITY/VOLUNTEER CONTRIBUTIONS

OTHERS

Legacy

What legacy do you wish to leave behind through your achievements and contributions?

Are there any current projects you are working on that will add to your legacy?

How would you like to impact your family, future generations, your community, and others?

Travel Adventures

TRAVEL ADVENTURES

The places we travel throughout our lives, domestically or internationally, can really change us. As we leave our footprints there, we also take learning and experience with us back home. In this way, your travels become part of your legacy.

This section of the book allows you to reflect on the places you've been and how those adventures have impacted your life. Be sure to consider local trips within your country, state or province as well as international travels.

You will also be given an opportunity to share where you've always wanted to go but haven't made it. Perhaps that will become a piece of unfinished business one of your loved ones will complete for you someday.

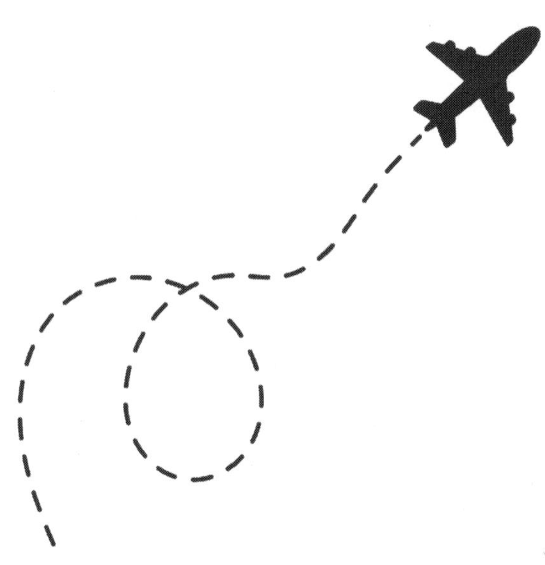

Where have your been?

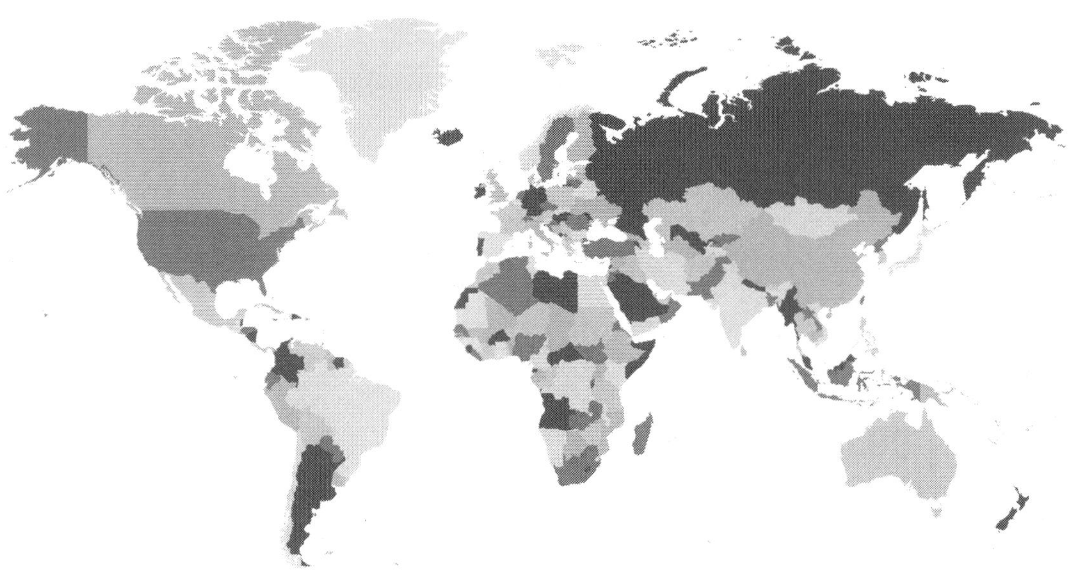

List all the places you have travelled including dates if desired. If it's been many, you might want to list just the countries, rather than cities, to make this task more manageable.

What was your most impactful trip? What happened? How did it change you?

What was your most fun trip? What did you do? Who was with you? What made is so memorable?

What was your most adventurous trip? What happened? How did it push you beyond your normal comfort zone?

Where would you like to go again and why?

Where would you like to go that you haven't been yet? and why?

What advice do you have for others that are wanting to travel?

Here are a few of my favorite trip photos...

A few more of my favorites travel pics...

Pivotal Moments

There are often several pivotal moments in one's life that alter our path in some way. This section of the book is to highlight those key turning points in various areas of your life.

You will explore life-altering events, career turns, personal transformations, perspective shifts, major relationship shifts, and spiritual awakenings. Instigators for these pivots could be things like losing a job, being in a major accident, health crisis, wars, pandemics, death of a loved one, birth of a child, or even mystical experiences.

Start thinking about those big happenings that created a shift in your life in some way and then continue on to complete this next section of the book.

Life-Altering Events

Were there any major life events or experiences (positive or negative) that changed the course of your life in some way. What happened? How did you navigate the experience? What was the outcome?

Career Path Turns

Identify specific moments or decisions that made significant changes to your career path. What happened? Where did it lead you? How did you navigate that change?

Personal Transformations

Identity any significant periods of personal growth in life? How did your perspective or priorities change? How did this shift affect others around you? How did it shift your sense of fulfillment in life?

Perspective Shifts

Did any significant events or situations cause a permanent shift to the way you view life or the people, places, and things within it? What was the instigating event? How did it change you?

Major Relationships Shifts

Did you experience any pivotal moments in relationships with others? How did it impact your relationship in a positive or negative way? What was the outcome.

Spiritual Awakenings

Have you had any spiritual awakenings or philosophical shifts that have reshaped your life in some way? What beliefs got transformed? How did it change the way you view of the world? How did it impact your sense of meaning and purpose?

Legacy Reflections

This a section to deeply reflect on your journey through life and the legacy you aspire to leave behind. It's a doorway into your mind and heart. Here you can share your aspirations for the future.

"You are creating your legacy every day by the actions that you take. Choose them consciously."
~Robin Harris, A Conscious Connection

Defining Your Legacy

How would you like to be remembered by future generations?

What specific contributions do you wish to be remembered for?

What values or principles do you want to be associated with and hope future generations will carry forward?

Impact On Others

What positive impact do you hope you made on others' lives?

How do you feel your influence has impacted those around you in a way that will continue into the future?

Are there any unresolved issues or relationships you would like to mend?

Lessons Learned

What important lessons learned would you like to pass on?

Do you have any regrets or things you wish you had done differently?

Gratitude

What have you appreciated the most about your life?

What or who are you most grateful for?

Purpose & Meaning

What have you discovered about the purpose and meaning of life?

In what areas have you found fulfillment in your life?

Legacy photos and mementos...

Final Thoughts

Other Additions

Add anything else you would like to tell about your life story that hasn't been said yet.

This Project Reflections

How do you feel about completing this project?

Memories Preserved

Family Recipe

Recipe Name

Serving

Prep Time

Cook Time

Ingredients

Directions

Notes

Family Recipe

Recipe Name

Serving

Prep Time

Cook Time

Ingredients

Directions

Notes

Family Recipe

Recipe Name

Serving

Prep Time

Cook Time

Ingredients

Directions

Notes

Family Recipe

Recipe Name

Serving

Prep Time

Cook Time

Ingredients

Directions

Notes

Ideas

The following ideas and information I want to share with the next generation. (Ex. a business idea you never got to bring to life, a discovery you've made, a new philosophy, etc.)

Things I Saved

Include newspaper clippings, pamphlets, certificates, pictures your kids created, etc. All those things you saved.

Things I Saved

Things I Saved

Things I Saved

Important Documents

Include important papers, documents, certificates, etc that may be useful to the future generations.

Important Documents

Notes to Loved Ones

The truth about life and relationships is that many things don't get said and many that do fade with time.

Way too often things get left unsaid in life. Perhaps we couldn't find the words to say them out loud. Perhaps we assumed the other person knew how we felt or what we thought.

Maybe there are important things we want remembered and although they've been said before, the passage of time has a way of fading things.

Writing a letter to loved ones is a way to deliver the words of our mind and feelings in our heart.

This section of the book has letter pages in which you can choose to write to whomever you choose. An opportunity to leave nothing unsaid nor forgotten.

Dear,

Dear,

Dear,

Dear,

Dear,

Dear,

Dear,

Dear,

Dear,

Dear,

Afterwards

Additions

A few pages have been added to the end of this book so you can capture additional thoughts, and add memories that may have happened after you've completed the book. Use this space however it works best for you. Write. Add pictures. Press your favorite flower.

Additions

Additions

Additions

This book was created by Conscious Minds Press.

Publisher of tools to help live a consciously connected, healthy, and aware life. Journals, Log books, Notebooks, Guides, Workbooks and more to support you and those you love.

Please consider leaving us a review on Amazon. Your positive feedback supports visibility of small independent publishers like us and encourages others to also invest in helpful tools for a conscious & connected life.

(Find the book title in your order history or in main search and click 'submit a product review'.)

Thank you kindly.

Find the complete
Story of My Life (book series) on Amazon:

Made in United States
Troutdale, OR
12/30/2024